AF504682

SUCCESS IS YOURS IN AFFILIATE MARKETING IF DEADLY MISTAKES KILLED

IDENTIFY AND AVOID MISTAKES

RAJESH KUMAR GIRI

Copyright © Rajesh Kumar Giri
All Rights Reserved.

ISBN 979-888629144-5

This book has been published with all efforts taken to make the material error-free after the consent of the author. However, the author and the publisher do not assume and hereby disclaim any liability to any party for any loss, damage, or disruption caused by errors or omissions, whether such errors or omissions result from negligence, accident, or any other cause.

While every effort has been made to avoid any mistake or omission, this publication is being sold on the condition and understanding that neither the author nor the publishers or printers would be liable in any manner to any person by reason of any mistake or omission in this publication or for any action taken or omitted to be taken or advice rendered or accepted on the basis of this work. For any defect in printing or binding the publishers will be liable only to replace the defective copy by another copy of this work then available.

Contents

Preface

> *""Nothing is impossible if an action is taken with desire, dedication and determination to learn before implement."*

As mistakes are common to all, then of course new affiliate marketers are not an exception. But learning from the mistakes of successful affiliate marketers will make a smooth passage to get skilled in "How to Avoid Killing Deadly Mistakes?" to achieve success with passive income goal.

The e-book is the result of skills and experiences acquired by practical knowledge in affiliate marketing for years. It is full of expertise as step-by-step guidance written in easy to understand language. Even beginners in affiliate marketing can kick-start building credibility, revenue and growth like a pro.

All books with similar topics look alike, but presentation and skills of making concepts clear are unique.

- Easy to understand language
- Clear-cut reasons, queries and resolution
- Step-by-step guidance to escalate the process
- Clear your why and how smoothly
- Special Expertise Tips

The e-book will certainly prove its worth as solution of affiliate marketing beginner's hurdles and their solution.

Disclaimer - The link as recommendation of services contain affiliate links.

Thanks

Rajesh Kumar Giri

(The Practical Success Coach)

Acknowledgements

Copyright @2021 All rights reserved

Author- Rajesh Kumar Giri

Rajesh Kumar Giri – The Practical Success Coach and the author has tried his best in the presentation of data, facts and information up-to-date. However he makes no claim or warranty implied to accuracy, applicability or complete information.

The author or the publisher is not liable for any loss or other damages that may occur as a result of any information in the eBook. All information in the eBook is protected under international copyright laws. Attempt to illegally reprint or distribute it is strictly prohibited and will be prosecuted fullest extent of laws.

This eBook is not intended for use as a source of legal, business, accounting or financial advice. All readers are advised to seek services of competent professionals in legal, business, accounting, and finance field.

You are encouraged to print this book for easy reading.

You have purchased e eBook for your own use, and you do not have the license to reprint or distribute it to anyone else.

Author/Publisher

Foreword

Opening Talk with Rajesh

Undoubtedly each person on the planet wishes to be successful and yearns for top position. But few of them achieve whatever they fix as goal in life.

Isn't it?

But

> *""Success and failure are aspects of life. So both should be accepted. Failures give another chance to learn more and get skilled better. It offers an opportunity indirectly to track and analyze the mistakes done that lead to lose".*"

It is a universal truth and works awesome for "Affiliate Marketing". Amazingly the failure rate in affiliate marketing is very high. 95% of the newbies fail to sustain more than three months.

Reasons are very simple as for example –

- High expectation
- Lack of patience
- Lack of learning & skill developing attitude.
- Badly in need of instant money for survival and
- Deadly common mistakes

> *""Making mistakes are common to all. But some of them learn before implement from the failures and mistakes of affiliate marketers".*"

To support your smooth journey in expansion and building sustainable foundation of affiliate marketing; you have to keep winning mindset. Just begins with thefact that 5% of affiliates are still successful and you'll be one of them.

Are you ready?

If your answer is "Yes"

Then let us start with deadly mistakes in affiliate marketing that kill the dream, revenue and career.

This book will be certainly masterpiece collection of experiences which will eliminate steps of mistakes with right action to take.

CHAPTER ONE

Don't Quit Affiliate Marketing Before Reading It

Let us start with the burning and hot questions.

"Why does 95% of newbie affiliates fail and quit affiliate marketing earlier?

And

"How may affiliate become success to be the part of 5% successful affiliate marketers?

The answer –

Deadly common mistakes and wrong mindset are the main reasons of failure of 95% of the affiliate marketers. Quitting in hurry is other.

But,

One can be the part of 5% successful people by eliminating such killing common mistakes.

Of course, affiliate program is one of the best techniques to monetize blog or website to generate extra revenue as traditional facts. Though in the new era there are several innovative and proven systems to become successful.

Example –

- Social media like Facebook, twitter etc
- YouTube channel
- Product reviews posts
- Whatsapp group posts etc

In spite of lots of tools and automated services unexpected failure rate of 95% cannot be denied.

There are several solid reasons behind the failure of affiliates/marketers. Some of them has mentioned in the book.

First of all begin with an introduction of affiliate marketing.

"Affiliate marketing is performance based model of advertising in which a company or an individual pay the affiliates or partners for generation of sales as commission".

To clear your basics do read eBook - "Basics to Pro Hacks Making Affiliate Marketing Work for You In 2022"

Right, the book reveals the facts with a precise and to the point lesson to start affiliate marketing for success rather than failure.

It also raises the curtain from the face of affiliate marketing in your mind as easy to do a business. Because it is all about selling. So be clear it requires effort, time, skill and patience.

"Reading habit is the only tool to identify the common mistakes of affiliate marketers. If once you identify them; it is easy to correct them avoiding their uses in your campaigns".

The most common mistakes made by newbies even professional affiliate marketers are revealed in the content.

You'll learn how to keep away yourself from those mistakes to become successful to write your own golden history of success.....

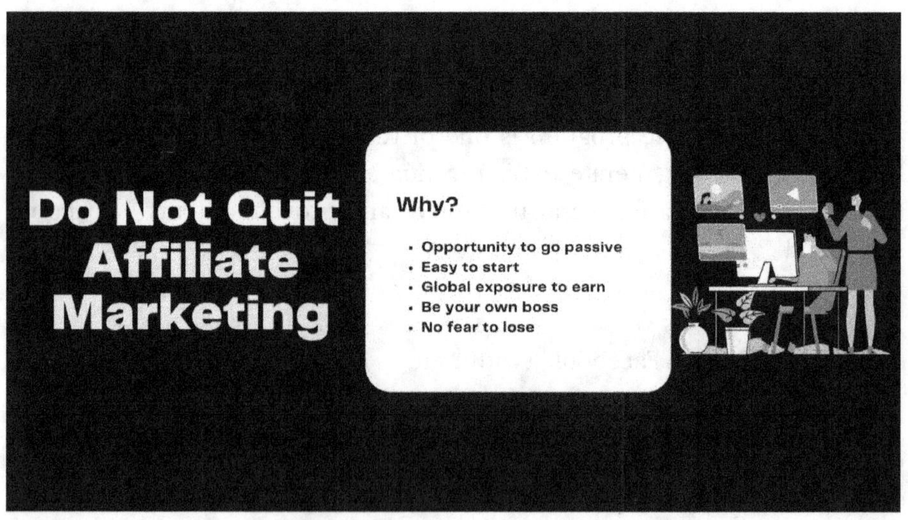

CHAPTER TWO

Start up Without Plan, Strategy and Goal

The fact that money drives people applies here. In affiliate marketing most of the failures start up promoting products or services without plan and strategy.

""Plan is outline of strategy that the affiliate marketer has to apply from first to final step for success".*"*

As per affiliate marketing blue print from my experiences the follow steps should be taken with strategy:-

1 Plan: Hosting a blog or website

Strategy – Start up with a blog with self-created quality and unique contents under niche.

2 Plan: Selection of hosting provider and budget

Strategy – Opt a pocket friendly hosting with 100% up time and best customer support.

3 Plan: E-mail Auto responder service

Strategy – It's not possible to reply visitors or email subscribers on daily basis manually, so an auto responder like Getresponse should be subscribed.

4 Plan: Market research, target audience and competitors: -Affiliate marketers should be aware of market, target audience under the niche and competitors.

Strategy – Read testimonials, research the market's demand and compare your brand with other competitors in the market. Finally make a clear cut strategy to go forward.

5 Plan: Clear cut objectives of your goal: -It's not enough to be clear about your monetary achievement; you have to know how to get it.

Strategy – Goals and their objectives must be clear.

- Revenue goals
- Cost and profitability
- Traffic
- Productivity
- Overcome technical challenges

Mistake – 5

Affiliate marketers don't care or underestimate the potential of clear and solid plan with strategy.

Solution:

Clear cut solid plan enhances affiliate marketing business that leads to success.

- Craft the perfect affiliate marketing strategy.
- Application of sophisticated strategies to earn more.

Special Bonus Tips: Quick checklists for kick start your affiliate marketing with plan and strategy.

- Right webhost and web design
- Genuine affiliate network selection
- Make SEO strategy
- Selection of niche
- Creation of engaging content
- Social media marketing strategy
- Opting best email auto responder

Recommendation – Getresponse is an excellent auto responder with multi-purpose uses as per my experience.

Free trial link – Free trial of Getresponse auto responder

CHAPTER THREE

Chance upon Selling Rather Than Focusing On Helping

"Helping people to get solution of their issues are billion dollars industry i.e Google, but affiliate marketers focus on sell first and fail".

""We should not underestimate the power of relationship. It is an awesome way to gain faith and confidence of visitors. People don't visit blog links to follow. They return to learn more from your content and expertise"."

"Affiliate marketing is the business of fostering relationship with people to bring traffic that turns to conversion".

Build relationship truly and friendly with

- Right and efficient partners
- Your contents by updating regularly to keep them up to date and fresh.
- Innovative tools
- Tracking and analysis

Mistake – 1

By default, the main goals of newbie affiliate marketers are to make sales to earn order to make their survival. So they focus on selling rather than building relationship by helping and guiding to resolve issues or taking final decisions.

Solution

To add value to your affiliate offers you need to focus on helping your niche, no matter what you promote or offer.

Check – You're offering or marketing weight loss products.

It means you're helping people to get fit, healthy and perfect shape.

- Help with natural diet schedules
- Yoga and exercises – Tips and schedules etc

Take Another – If you're an affiliate with niche gadgets/YouTube accessories then you are helping people to find out best gadgets or YouTube accessories as per their need. You should start guiding free with –

- Best photography tips and tricks
- How to shoot HD shorts etc

Interact And Develop Relation

To be frank always focus on helping your target niche customers. It will help to build sound and firm repo. In result people will like to buy products clicking your affiliate links. Your goal of selling and increasing conversion rate will become easier than before.

""Once helping attitude evolves it'll become habit. Caring and helping habit always impress masses. Your achievement with repo could be increased"."

Special Bonus Tips:

- Strong relations are built on helpful and informative content
- Interaction plays significant role.

Trapped In Fast Money Making Investment Offers

Even if there are lots of affiliates programs that will make huge money but majorities of affiliate marketers are trapped in

- Fast money making
- Get-rich-quick-scheme
- Make money online etc

Money Making Online Schemes

Without a doubt such money making online program is one of the most lucrative business financially. But such programs have recruit limitations and no quality products to sell. So even reaching entire market place virtually there would be nothing to sell. Finally no way to add new value.

Mistake – 2

Instead of investing time in leaning researching and developing skill affiliate marketers join wrong, easy to promote or money making affiliate program and failed or quit after losing reputation, money and their precious time.

Solution

Join the affiliate program after research and asking some question yourself?

- "What do you have passion for?
- What is it that I like to buy or use?
- What is my expertise?
- What are my interests?
- Can I recommend the product or offers to friend and family?

Positive and self – satisfactory answers will help to take firm decision to opt the niche to start affiliate marketing.

"Start working with passion in your opted niche you love and have expertise. Then success cannot be denied".

""Every person has own passion and interest that can be turned into profit if action is taken with skill"."

Special Bonus Tip: - If the affiliate network charges fee to promote their products or services then stay away. Such programs may be scam or based on Multi-level Marketing model and disguised as affiliate program.

CHAPTER FIVE

Trials with Multiple Niches

Hey reader!

Do you remember the quote?

Catching two or more rabbits a time means losing all.

But here, the scenario is different. Affiliate marketers start to try with multiple niches and unwillingly become competitor of millions of revenue hungry people called affiliates.

"I love competitions but mind it competitions should be fair".

In spite of tons of opportunities majority of affiliate marketers follow masses and copy –

- Click hungry content creators
- Views like and comment seeking YouTube creators.
- Social media influencers etc

Starting With Multiple Niches Leads To Failure

In result they start with the mindset that affiliate marketing means sign up and promote link to earn without making efforts.

So the more affiliate program one joins the more revenue one's generate. The mindset of "More Affiliate Programs More Income" makes a dark way that leads to failure.

Mistake – 3

Affiliate marketers get trapped to join so many affiliate programs for more income and failed to manage all. They did not get expected results and get frustrated.

> *"Temptation to generate more revenue; results in spreading too thin by new affiliate marketers by joining in so many affiliate networks".*

To manage multiple blogs, products, email lists, queries resolution, accounts social media interactions etc and invest required time in research, product knowledge and creating contents etc that are basics to develop network; become tougher and create distraction.

Solution:-

The affiliate marketer should begin with one or two key niches as their experiences and interest.

""Focus on a niche at a time until you master the affiliate's techniques"."

Focus on your niche and work with dedication to bring decent traffic

- Grow e-mail list
- Create social media presence with difference making attitude
- Build friendly relations with social media fans
- Put enough effort to make a real difference in the niche

""Trust the leaders of the affiliate marketing industry. They're sticking with Legimate affiliate programs of popular and reputed companies for years. That's why they are earning huge and passive income"."

The best way to be successful in affiliate marketing is to promote two or more products from one affiliate network with your content niche.

Special Bonus Tip: "The best way to be successful in affiliate marketing is to promote two or more products from one affiliate network with your content niche".

CHAPTER SIX

Lack of Product Knowledge as Testing or Self-Use Ignored

"It is impossible to outline unique authentic and useful information about a product that you've never used or tested yourself".

Yes,

Lack of product knowledge is also the major cause of failure in affiliate marketing.

Majority of affiliates don't buy and test the product they promote. They have mindset that products can be sold only providing apparent information and superficial features.

Keep in mind the visitors returns to your blog or website, only if they get reliable knowledge. It is possible to give if you become by product of the product.

Exceptions are never taken as an example. There are some products i.e (Medicines) or Supplements related to specific health issue cannot be tested if you're not suffering from it.

Mistake – 4

To generate quick revenue and increase conversion rate affiliates join the affiliate network without using, testing and researching the product/ service.

Solution:

There is not hidden secret except use of product to speak about its features, benefits and side effects.

- Purchase the product
- Use it yourself
- Experience its benefits and side-effects if any
- Create a content expressing "How the product changed your life".
- Compare with other products in the market
- Leave your review on other blogs under the product niche with your blog link.

Special Bonus Tips: -

You are CEO of your niche blog contents and its reputation. So select ultimate and result – oriented product to promote. Use it to experience its result. Review yourself then your confidence and trust will advocate you words in recommendation.

CHAPTER SEVEN

Selection of Wrong Affiliate Program Network

"All affiliate network programs in an industry niche look alike but mind the fact, those are not created equally."

Selection of the right affiliate network can be a daunting task.

Remember

It does not matter how expert you are in affiliate marketing, but if you do not start with reputed affiliate network program then you will lose your repo.

Most of beginners wish to earn money from affiliate marketing quickly. So, they trap in high commission paying program. They do not research its pros and cons. Even they fail to track trends and demands of products.

Resultantly they do not generate expected revenue and become frustrate. Ultimately quit it earlier and fail.

When trying to choose the right affiliate network, it's important to focus on four key factors:

- The monetary value of what you are selling.
- Customer service and support provided by the affiliate network.
- Result of the product from testimonials.
- The payout you receive for your affiliate sales.

There are so many affiliate networks available online. The issue with choosing the right one is that you need to know what is really important.

However, there are some tips you should always follow when it comes to affiliate marketing.

It is all about the products you can sell to your customers. You need to choose a network that offers you high-quality products, and it also means choosing an affiliate network that will give you good rewards for your work.

A great product with high quality is always appealing to many consumers. If you want to earn money with affiliate marketing or blogging platform, you need to know that the majority of people are looking for products of the best quality.

Features to check to join an affiliate program

Help and fit for niche audience

Begin with researching the product and services that may help and is fit for your niche audience.

Check what kind of products can you recommend?

It means you have to find out what your audience need to get their lives better like

- Fat to fit – weight loss
- Beautify skin – anti – ageing solution
- Webhosting or SEO tools etc

Never choose an affiliate program just for high commission. May be you earn but cannot sustain longer.

Outstanding Brand Repo

Opt an affiliate program that has outstanding brand reputation, high demand and high conversion rate.

Never join a plan paying subscription or membership fee.

- Research reading product reviews
- Go through latest customer reviews and comments
- Discuss in community and group about drawbacks
- Take community members opinion posting poll.

Promotional Tools and Resources

Always check promotional tools and resources before joining an affiliate program.

Best promotional tools and resources enhance the chances of more clicks with maximum conversions.

Check –

- Banner ads
- Landing pages
- Creative email templates
- Videos
- Learning resources
- Client testimonials etc

Conversion Rate and Payout

If your compensation in the form of commissions from affiliate marketing and blog posts isn't enough, then it might not be worth spending time and money on an affiliate program which doesn't offer enough rewards for every click on their website or blog post.

Affiliate marketing model works on cost-per-sale (CPS). So conversion rate matters to generate more revenue.

Ensure the rate of conversion before joining the affiliate program.

Mistake – 5

Most of beginners in affiliate marketing join an affiliate program just for commission. They do not use products. Depend solely on reading features and fabricated reviews online.

Solution:

Buy and try branded popular and high-quality product. Experience its benefit and compare with features. If it can solve a problem, then promote.

CHAPTER EIGHT

No Skill to Create Quality Content under Niche

Content is your stories of experiences. It is imagination, innermost thought and hopes to build a passive income with unparallel lifestyle. Put talent, sweat and tears in it to make it worth to pay.

""Creating high-quality and unique content is an art. The skill is compulsory for affiliate marketers to survive long term of course every individual is not a born writer but the skill can be developed by reading and writing." "

"In affiliate marketing quality and interesting as well as engaging content writing is not an option; it is compulsion that requires time energy, resources, skill and efforts"

Before creating a content be clear about

- Target audience
- Need of audience
- What unique words or knowledge you have to share
- How confident you're in describing facts
- Skill of your experience/ learning in presentation

Then

'How your content benefits or improves the life of a reader?

"Keyword research and its application in content also play vital role in the generation of organic traffic."

Mistake – 6

Most of the contents in the blogs or websites of new affiliate marketers are just a sales pitch to drive sales. Contents lack –

- In depth and authentic information
- Unable to make readers engage and feel like value addition
- Fails to convince that information worth learning

Solution:
Never create contents just for

- Traffic and sales
- To build brand
- To get more subscribes only. Try to present facts in unique way to engage reader to stay on blog longer with confidence that he'll learn something new.

Special Bonus Tips: Generally Google ranks a content with more than 2000 words on first page. So follow these tips to go on top.

- 5000 plus words in content
- Short paragraphs
- Table of contents (Chapters)
- Avoid spelling and grammar mistakes
- Follow the blogging format
- Avoid repetition of headlines
- Add images related to content
- Optimize text for SEO

How to Create High Quality Content?

"Creating high quality content is an art to assume oneself as the reader with queries and answering the questions or doubts based upon facts and data."

Most of the affiliate marketers stick on defining quality content on the basis of no. of words, visual appeal, format, keywords, facts, spelling and grammar etc.

But mind the fact that data speaks louder than factual ideas. So let us learn to master it.

- **Identification of search intent** – In general search intent is keywords or search phrases to find

- General information about a topic
- Answer of query
- Products feature, cost and benefits
- Solution of a problem etc.

So before creating content; clear it how people around the globe will find it.

- **Facts with data** – Research and use data to explain and verify the facts presented in content. Follow the traits within data quality like

- Accuracy
- Reliability
- Relevance
- Validity
- Timeline and
- Consistency etc.

- **Craft for users** – Share personal experiences or write a case-study to represent in depth information. Avoid click bait writing just to trap and entice visitors to surf website. It impacts inversely and unique follower is lost forever.
- **Avoid manipulation** – Never create contents to deceive users by manipulation or tricks to rank in search engines. Even Google warns to copy spin or use of tricks to manipulate contents. Sometime it results in penalty if the original content creator files complaint in DMCA.

[DMCA – Digital Millennium Copyright Act]

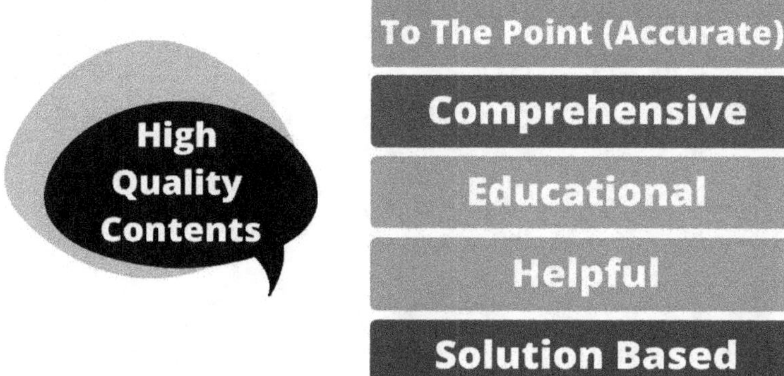

How to Check the Quality of Content

> *"Writing content is not enough. It must be compelling, to the point, informative and unique. The high quality of content means creating value and guarantees engagement of readers that results in more revenue. So it is compulsory to check its present value"*

6 points to check the quality of any content is commonly considered.

- **Informative or Sales Pitch** – Content must be informative rather than just a sales pitch to generate revenue.
- **Number of Words and Language** – Create the content in about 4000 plus words so that every required point can be discussed. Presentation of facts should be in easy to understand language.
- **Plagiarism** – Check whether the content is unique or not. Use plagiarism checker tools free or premium. Premium plagiarism checker is recommended to get 100% accurate result.
- **Keywords** – Use appropriate keywords in title, first paragraph and at least in one sub-heading.

- **Spelling and Grammar Check** – Check grammar and spelling carefully using grammar checking tools like Grammarly.
- **Data, Facts & Format** – Authenticity of facts and proper format should also be checked carefully.

Final Words Of Conclusion

Finally there are several other reasons too. But if affiliate is serious about making money and has started affiliate marketing with vision then just stick to it avoiding mistakes to succeed.

The newbies start affiliate marketing with great enthusiasm, but wrap up it with lots of negativity. Most of failure affiliates are those people who expect fast and easy earning without doing self-research and plan.

"The main reason of failure is to quit affiliate marketing earlier otherwise to neglect vital mistakes are easy by identifying them".

Hope the eBook's publishing purpose to guide to identify common mistakes and tips to avoid them is fulfilled so do not forget to review the eBook edition as comment.

Good luck!

www.ingramcontent.com/pod-product-compliance
Lightning Source LLC
Chambersburg PA
CBHW072145150726
48002CB00004B/1633